Phineas and FERB

SCIENCE LAB

Scholastic Inc.
New York Toronto London Auckland
Sydney Mexico City New Delhi Hong Kong

ISBN 978-0-545-37156-8

Based on the series created by Dan Povenmire and Jeff "Swampy" Marsh

12 11 10 9 8 7 6 5 4 3 2   11 12 13 14 15 16/0

First printing, October 2011
Printed and assembled in China

CONTENTS

*Words in bold throughout the book are defined here.

Ferb

Do YOU Know What You're Gonna Do TODAY?

Agent P

Phineas and Ferb know exactly what they're gonna do today! They are going to have some fun with science! Their backyard laboratory is all set up and ready to roll, but they're missing one key ingredient: YOU!

Help Phineas and Ferb tackle some totally spectacular experiments. You'll make things that will fizz, bubble, or even EXPLODE! But no matter what you do, make sure to be on the lookout for a couple of folks who are itching to ruin your experiments.

Candace, Phineas and Ferb's older sister, is constantly trying to bust her brothers by catching them doing something crazy.

Also, keep an eye out for the very evil **Dr. Doofenshmirtz**, the head of Doofenshmirtz Evil, Incorporated. He's trying to wreak havoc on the Tri-State Area.

But don't worry! **Perry**, Phineas and Ferb's pet platypus, has your back. *Shhh* . . . He's also known as **Agent P**, a secret agent with the O.W.C.A. (Organization Without a Cool Acronym). He's out to stop Dr. Doofenshmirtz.

Dr. Doofenshmirtz

Lab Gear

You need to haul some equipment to the backyard lab. To help you get started, this kit comes with the following:

- Glow-in-the-dark slime powder
- Tweezers
- 2 Test tubes
- 2 Test tube caps
- Dropper
- Petri dish
- 3 Strips of litmus paper
- Funnel

SLiME POWDeR

Candace

Super scooper measuring spoon:
This spoon has two ends. The large end holds ½ teaspoon of stuff and the smaller end holds ¼ teaspoon.

Lab station:
This thing contains *lots* of holes. The three deep, round wells are your test tube holders. Use the other wells to mix liquids and other stuff during your experiments.

Okay. Let's find Perry and head to the backyard. HEY, where's **PERRY?**

Alert! Alert!

What's one way to prevent Candace from getting you busted? By keeping your workspace clean and problem-free. Also, be sure to follow these simple guidelines:

- Stick to the instructions in this book. **Don't** try to alter the steps in any of the experiments. That could be dangerous! Don't try to make up new experiments, either. That is a safety risk, too.

- Get a pair of safety goggles from your local home improvement store. They help to protect your eyes while performing experiments.

- **Don't** eat or drink the results of the experiments. Any food items you use in your experiments should be thrown away at the end of the experiment.

- Wash your hands after each experiment.

- If the instructions tell you to get an adult helper, be sure to ask for help from a trusted adult. **DON'T** try the experiments on your own.

- Don't make a mess. Cover your work area with sheets of newspaper. Wear an apron or an old T-shirt you don't mind ruining.

Clean your tools after every experiment. If your tools are dirty, your experiments might not work.

It's safe to flush the liquids used in this book down the drain. Just let the faucet run until the sink is clean.

Don't flush any solid or semi-solid materials (like slime) down the drain. Put these things in a plastic bag and toss them into the trash can.

Some experiments will require you to use some common household objects. Be sure to ask an adult before you use any of these items!

Chemistry is always a blast . . .
just as long as you can avoid run-ins with
Candace. With these points in mind,

LET'S GET STARTED.

Dance, Dance, Dance!

What's that? You feel a song coming on? How about a dance! Phineas and Ferb love to dance. The boys can get anyone and anything (even a dish of milk) to bust a move. How? Let's find out!

What You Need:
- Petri dish
- Whole milk
- Dropper
- Food coloring
- Dishwashing liquid

What You Do:

1. Fill one Petri dish with milk and put the dish on a flat surface.

2. Use your liquid dropper to put a drop of food coloring into the milk.

3. Clean your dropper with water. Squeeze the bulb to pump water in and out.

4. Use your dropper to put one drop of dishwashing liquid on top of the food coloring.

5. Watch the food coloring as it swirls around madly. The milk will begin to dance all over the place!

More Stuff to Try

Think that was cool? You haven't seen anything yet! Fill a cookie sheet with a thin layer of whole milk. Dump in several drops of food coloring (use different colors, of course). Space them evenly around the edges of the cookie sheet. Put one drop of dishwashing liquid on each dot of food coloring.

WHOA!

What's Happening Here?

Whole milk contains both water and fat. These substances can't bind to each other. Dishwashing liquid, however, *is* attracted to the fat. Millions of rapid connections between soap **molecules** and fat molecules make the milk move. The food coloring allows you to see the milk bust out some swirly action. If you're lucky, the dance show might last as long as half an hour!

Not a Good Mix

Phineas and Ferb just don't blend with their sister, Candace. She's always trying to bust them for *something*. If the boys were water, Candace would have to be oil. Hey, that sounds like a great experiment! See for yourself how these two liquids refuse to mix.

⚠ WARNING
Food coloring can stain. Use with caution.

What You Need:
- Disposable cup
- Water
- Blue food coloring
- Test tube and cap
- Lab station
- Funnel
- Vegetable oil
- Clear tape

What You Do:

1. Fill the cup with cold tap water.

2. Add a few drops of blue food coloring to the water. Swirl the cup to mix.

3. Put the test tube into its stand in the lab station. Use the funnel to fill the test tube halfway full with blue water.

4. Very slowly and carefully fill the rest of the test tube with vegetable oil. Hey, check it out! The oil is sitting RIGHT ON TOP of the water!

5. Put a cap on the test tube. Wrap tape around the bottom cap to seal it. Gently turn the test tube upside down. WOW! The water oozes downward as a big blue blob!

The oil in the test tube is just like Candace—always hovering over Phineas and Ferb! Want to check out something else that's pretty cool? Flip the test tube up and down a few times. The big blue blob will separate into several smaller blobs. Now, hold on to the cap and shake the test tube for ten seconds. See what happens!

What's Happening Here?

Water has a greater **density** than oil. This means that a certain amount of water weighs more than the same amount of oil. For this reason, oil floats on top of water. When you flip your test tube upside down, you very briefly reverse the position of the two liquids. The heavy water soon falls back to the bottom of the test tube. Also, water and oil are **immiscible**, which means they can't mix—no matter how much you stir or shake them.

Instant Balloon Inflator

Agent P just received word that Dr. Doofenshmirtz is building a hot-air balloon to give him a bird's eye view of the Tri-State Area. But no worries! Agent P has a few tricks of his own. In this experiment, help Agent P distract Dr. Doofenshmirtz by creating a balloon that can inflate by itself!

⚠ WARNING

This experiment can get messy. It's best to work near a sink.

What You Need:

- Lab station
- Test tube
- Vinegar
- Small round balloon
- Funnel
- 1 teaspoon baking soda

What You Do:

1. Put your test tube in the test-tube holder. Make sure it's standing straight and secure.

2. Carefully fill the test tube halfway full with vinegar.

3. Put the tip of the funnel into the mouth of the balloon. Pour the baking soda through the funnel, into the balloon.

4. Shake the baking soda into the bottom of the balloon. Stretch the mouth of the balloon over the test tube, making sure the baking soda doesn't spill into the test tube.

5. When the balloon is securely over the test tube, lift the balloon and shake the baking soda out into the test tube.

6. Watch your balloon inflate! (If the balloon does not begin to inflate, softly shake the test tube to fully dissolve the contents inside.)

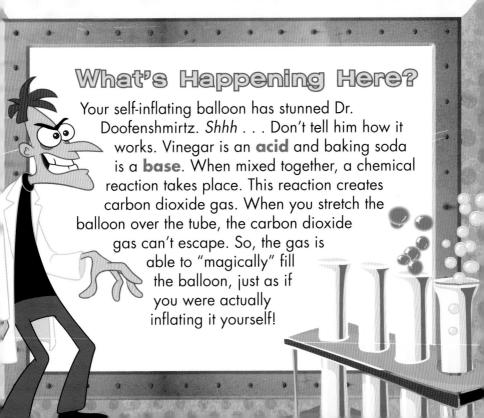

What's Happening Here?

Your self-inflating balloon has stunned Dr. Doofenshmirtz. *Shhh . . .* Don't tell him how it works. Vinegar is an **acid** and baking soda is a **base**. When mixed together, a chemical reaction takes place. This reaction creates carbon dioxide gas. When you stretch the balloon over the tube, the carbon dioxide gas can't escape. So, the gas is able to "magically" fill the balloon, just as if you were actually inflating it yourself!

Acid Tester

Agent P needs to find an acid to destroy Dr. Doofenshmirtz's newest evil invention. Let's help him find one!

What You Need:
- Old newspaper
- Litmus paper
- Dropper
- 3 types of a household liquid (vinegar, hand soap, shampoo, lemon juice, window cleaner, clear soda, etc.)

NEWS

What You Do:

1. Spread the newspaper over your work area.

2. Lay a strip of litmus paper on the newspaper.

3. Use the dropper to put one drop of household liquid on a section of the litmus paper.

4. Flush the dropper with water.

5. Repeat Steps 3 and 4 for the two remaining liquids.

6. Compare the color blotches on the paper to the pH color chart. The lower the number in the chart, the stronger the acid.

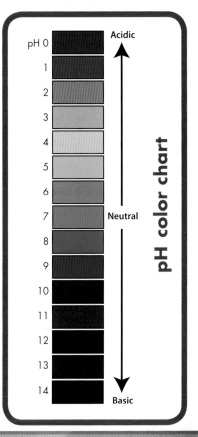

Acidic

pH 0
1
2
3
4
5
6
7   Neutral
8
9
10
11
12
13
14   Basic

pH color chart

What's Happening Here?

HEY! Not only can you tell an acid from a base, you can see how strong each substance is. Cool! How does litmus paper work? Well, the paper contains dyes that change colors when they touch **hydrogen** and **hydroxide ions**. Acids contain hydrogen ions, and bases contain hydroxide ions. When you drop substances onto the litmus paper, the different amounts and types of ions in each substance turn the paper different colors.

Ghost Sighting

Agent P is talking to Major Monogram, his commanding officer at the O.W.C.A. They are discussing different ways to scare Dr. Doofenshmirtz. What's that, Agent P? You're going to make a ghost? What a great idea! Dr. Doofenshmirtz will *never* be able to take over the Tri-State Area if he thinks a ghost is haunting him!

Major Monogram

!WARNING

This experiment can get messy. Work near a sink, and spread newspaper over your work area. Don't forget: Food coloring can stain!

What You Need:

- Adult helper
- Food coloring (any dark color)
- Disposable cup filled with warm water
- 2 test tubes
- Funnel
- Cold water
- Index card

What You Do:

1. Mix several drops of food coloring with the warm water in the cup.

2. Ask your adult helper to hold one of the test tubes. Use the funnel to fill the test tube to the top with the colored warm water.

3. Rinse the funnel. Use it to fill the other test tube to the rim with cold water. Cover the test tube's opening with the index card.

4. Holding the index card in place, carefully turn the cold-water-filled test tube upside down. Set the card and the test tube on the warm-water-filled test tube that your helper is holding. Make sure the openings of the two test tubes line up EXACTLY.

5. Keep holding the test tubes so they won't shift. Then, carefully slide the index card out from between the tubes. YIKES! The GHOST in the bottom test tube is rising.

What's Happening Here?

Warm water is less dense than cold water. When you remove the index card, the warm water in the bottom test tube rises. At the same time, the cold water in the top test tube drops to the bottom. The coloring of the warm water allows you to see the process in action.

Underwater Kaboom

Agent P just received word that Dr. Doofenshmirtz wants to invent a machine that destroys fireworks. He plans to use it to ruin the Fourth of July. No worries! Phineas and Ferb have invented underwater fireworks! Dr. Doofenshmirtz will never expect these colorful, underwater explosions.

What You Need:
- 1 tablespoon food coloring (any color)
- 1 tablespoon cooking oil
- Small mixing bowl
- Spoon
- Dropper
- Large, clear glass filled with water

What You Do:

1. Put the food coloring and the cooking oil in the mixing bowl.

2. Use the spoon to mix the color and oil.

3. Fill the dropper with the colored oil.

4. Dip the tip of the dropper under the water level in the glass.

5. Release one drop of the oil mixture into the water. What do you see?

6. Can't believe your eyes? Release another drop. Wow!

What's Happening Here?

When you drop food coloring by itself into water, the color spreads almost immediately. This is called **diffusion**. But if you've ever dropped oil into water, you've probably noticed that the two substances don't mix. By mixing the food coloring with oil before dropping it into the water, the food coloring briefly gets a waterproof shield from the oil. As the oil and food coloring move against each other in the water, the food coloring eventually works its way through the oil and comes in contact with the water. Result: An explosive "firework" of color! What a blast!

Slime Time!

There is one thing that Phineas and Ferb know will make every day more exciting. That one thing is slime, especially if it glows in the dark! There's no hidden trick to this experiment, just SLIME!

SLiME POWDeR

What You Need:
- Lab station
- Glow-in-the-dark slime powder
- Measuring spoon
- Warm water

What You Do:

1. Put 1¼ teaspoons of slime powder into the large well in your lab station. (Don't use the whole pack. You need to save the other half for the next experiment.)

2. Add 6 teaspoons of warm water to the lab compartment. Stir the mixture with your finger until all of the powder dissolves. If the slime feels too clumpy, add another ½ teaspoon of warm water.

3. Once your mixture is nice and gooey, dig in and play with your slime! Squish it and see how it behaves. If the slime begins to feel dry, add another ½ teaspoon of warm water.

4. Now, switch off the light and see the slime glow. Creepy!

What's Happening Here?

Slime behaves like a liquid when it's oozing in your hand, but it becomes firmer when squeezed. That's because slime is a **polymer**, or substance made up of long, chainlike molecules. When you squeeze the slime, the molecules become tangled. That's why the slime stiffens. This slime is extra special because it glows in the dark. It contains a material that absorbs light energy. When you take the slime into a dark place, it starts to release the energy it absorbed. The released energy can be seen as visible light. This is called **phosphorescence**. Over time, the slime releases most of its stored energy, causing the glow to fade. But don't worry, you can recharge the slime by exposing it to light.

Exploding Slime

Oh no! Candace is on to your slimy experimentations. She's about to tell MOM! Quick, make the rest of your slime powder disappear. Or, better yet, EXPLODE!

! WARNING

Have an adult helper give you a hand. This can get messy. Make sure you work near a sink. Line your work surface with newspaper!

What You Need:

- Lab station
- 2 test tubes
- Dropper
- Vinegar
- Dishwashing liquid
- Baking soda
- Petri dish
- Measuring spoon
- Glow-in-the-dark slime powder
- Funnel

What You Do:

1. Set one test tube into a stand in the lab station.

2. Carefully fill the test tube to the four-milliliter mark with water. Then add three drops of dishwashing liquid into the water.

3. Put ¼ teaspoon of baking soda and ¼ teaspoon of the slime powder into the Petri dish. Mix well.

4. Use the funnel to pour the powder mixture into the test tube. Put the cap on the test tube and shake until the ingredients are fully mixed.

5. Fill the dropper with vinegar.

6. Remove the cap from your test tube, and, 1, 2, 3… squeeze the vinegar into the test tube and watch what happens!

What's Happening Here?

Poof! Like the experiment on page 12, the vinegar (acid) reacts with the baking soda (base), causing a chemical reaction. This reaction creates carbon dioxide gas, which causes the liquid mixture inside the tube to bubble up and erupt. The dish soap adds extra bubbly action. The slime powder causes the eruption to be extra slimy!

Mystery Blob

Because of Candace, Phineas and Ferb are all out of slime powder. What are they going to do? Luckily Phineas had an idea. They'll make some homemade slime!

What You Need:
- Lab station
- Test tube
- Water
- Bowl
- Measuring spoon
- Cornstarch

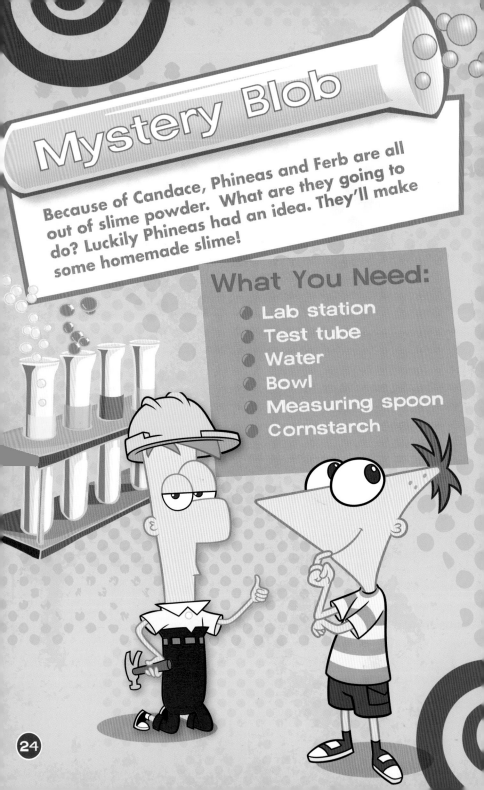

What You Do:

1. Fill the test tube to the 10-milliliter mark with water. Then pour it into the large well in your lab station.

2. Repeat one more time.

3. Add a level teaspoonful of cornstarch to the water and stir. Keep adding a little cornstarch and stirring until you have a slime that runs slowly when you tip the bowl.

4. Pick up the slime and squeeze it. Gross!

What's Happening Here?

Candace will never suspect where your mystery blob came from! This slime is just like the one from the experiment on page 20. It is runny like a liquid until you squeeze it. Then it stiffens. That's because slime, a polymer, is made up of long, chainlike molecules. When you squeeze the slime, the molecules link together.

More Stuff to Try

Color your blob! Just mix in some of your favorite food coloring.

⚠ WARNING!
Food coloring can stain.

Money Disguiser

Oh no! Dr. Doofenshmirtz wants to invent a machine that snatches kids' lunch money. Wait! Agent P has a plan. He's going to disguise money so Dr. Doofenshmirtz can't find it! Great thinking, Agent P.

What You Need:
- Paper towel
- Petri dish
- Vinegar
- A few pennies
- Tweezers

What You Do:

1. Fold the paper towel in half, and then in half again.

2. Put the folded paper towel in the Petri dish.

3. Pour enough vinegar into the Petri dish to wet the paper towel.

4. Cover the paper towel with pennies.

5. Let the pennies sit for 24 hours. Don't be tempted to touch them!

6. After 24 hours, use the tweezers to pick up each penny for a closer look. What do you see?

What's Happening Here?

Agent P's a master of disguises. What's this disguise made of? Vinegar is an acid. When it combines with the copper in the pennies, a chemical reaction takes place, causing a green coating made of copper acetate to form on the pennies.

More Stuff to Try

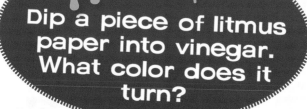

Dip a piece of litmus paper into vinegar. What color does it turn?

Sink or Swim?

Here comes Isabella Garcia-Shapiro, Phineas and Ferb's friend and neighbor. She's always asking, "Whatcha doin'?" The boys are always ready to have her help out with their experiments. Look! They just made a bag of rocks float above Isabella's head. Let's see what other things they can make float.

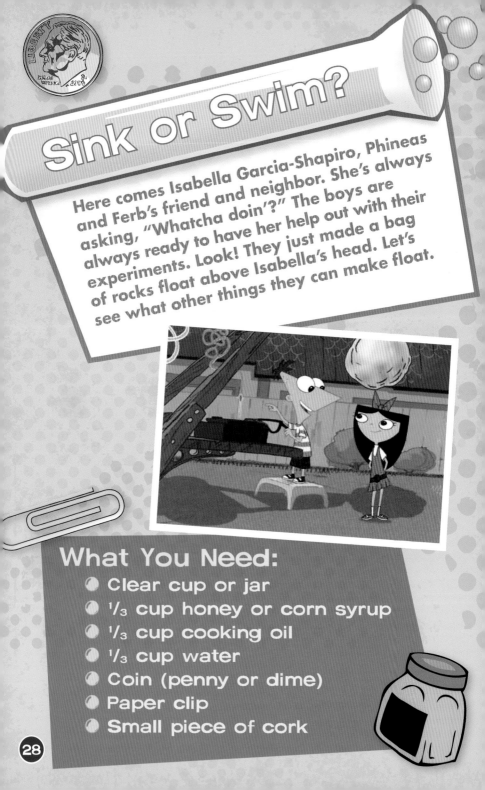

What You Need:

- Clear cup or jar
- 1/3 cup honey or corn syrup
- 1/3 cup cooking oil
- 1/3 cup water
- Coin (penny or dime)
- Paper clip
- Small piece of cork

What You Do:

1. Put the cup on a flat surface.

2. Pour the honey or corn syrup into the cup.

3. Pour cooking oil into the cup. Finally, add water.

4. Allow the liquid to settle into three layers. Cool, huh?

5. Drop the coin, paper clip, and cork into the cup. What happens?

What's Happening Here?

Remember the activity on page 10? Like that one, this activity is all about density. The difference in density causes the water to float to the top, the cooking oil to sit in the middle, and the corn syrup or honey to sink to the bottom. The objects you throw into the cup have different densities, too. Each one sinks to the level of the liquid that has a density greater than the object itself.

Build Your Own Mini Hovercraft

You spent the whole day working in Phineas and Ferb's backyard lab. You learned some awesome things about science. And you dodged Candace! How do you top that? Build a hovercraft to ride home!

⚠ WARNING

This experiment requires using (and ruining) a CD. Ask an adult helper to provide you with a CD that they don't mind you destroying. Do NOT take a CD without permission.

What You Need:

- CD
- Water bottle lid with a pop-up spigot
- Glue
- Medium-sized balloon

What You Do:

1. Close the spigot on the bottle lid. Then place the non-spigot side of the lid over the hole in the center of the CD.

2. Glue the bottom of the lid to the CD. Let the glue dry completely. Be patient!

3. Blow up the balloon. Pinch the neck so no air escapes.

4. Carefully stretch the neck of the balloon over the closed spigot.

5. Place your hovercraft on a smooth surface, such as a tabletop. Push it. What happens? Nothing? Don't worry, that was just a test run.

6. Now, keep the CD on the flat surface and open the spigot—make sure the balloon stays attached. Push the CD and watch your hovercraft go!

Wheeeeeeee!

What's Happening Here?

During the test run, the CD rubs against the surface. This generates **friction**, a rubbing force that slows down moving objects. Opening the spigot allows air from the balloon to flow under the CD. The air lifts the CD and keeps it from rubbing against the surface.
Result: No friction to slow down the hovercraft!

GLOSSARY

ACID: Liquid that is usually characterized as having a sour taste. Acid contains an excess of hydrogen ions, or electrically charged particles.

ATOM: Smallest possible particle of a chemical element

BASE: Any chemical compound that gives off negatively charged hydroxide ions when dissolved in water. Bases react with acids to form neutral substances.

DENSITY: Amount of **mass** in a given unit

DIFFUSION: Act of dispersing or spreading out

FRICTION: Slowing force that results from two objects rubbing against each other

HYDROGEN: An invisible, odorless gas. Hydrogen is the most common element in the universe.

HYDROXIDE ION: Negatively charged **ion** made of one hydrogen **atom** and one oxygen atom

IMMISCIBLE: Unable to dissolve in each other

ION: Any atom or group of atoms that has an unequal number of protons (positively charged particles) and electrons (negatively charged particles)

MASS: Amount of matter in an object

MOLECULE: Neutral group of two or more atoms

PHOSPHORESCENCE: When an object gives off light that it has absorbed

POLYMER: Compound made of long, chainlike molecules